Ramsbury
— Then and Now —

Barbara Croucher

First published 1995.
Published by BARBARA CROUCHER, 25 Ashley Piece, Ramsbury,
Marlborough, Wiltshire SN8 2QE.
ISBN 0-9511293-1-7

Printed in Singapore.

A catalogue record for this book is available from the British Library.

Design: Wendy Bann
Cover design: Denis Holland
Cartography: Margaret Chaplin

Typesetting by Duncan Croucher, 25 Ashley Piece, Ramsbury,
Marlborough, Wiltshire SN8 2QE

Printed by Hugh Stancliffe Associates, PO Box 113, Marlborough,
Wiltshire SN8 1RL and Eurasia Press, Singapore

The author and publishers have made every effort to trace the copyright holders
but if they have inadvertantly overlooked any, they will be pleased
to make the necessary arrangements at the first opportunity.

Front cover: Colour Barbara Croucher 1994, b/w WCC Local Studies
               Frith collection 1950s
Back cover: Peter Mills 1962

Contents

DEDICATION
To the villagers of Ramsbury, both past and present

ACKNOWLEDGEMENTS

Although over the years I have built up a large collection of photographs, in order to produce this book I have been indebted to many people for kindly lending me their photographs to supplement mine. I am especially grateful to the following: Steve Alder, Maria Barrett, Simon Blunt, Georgie Brooks, John Day, Brian Hale, Michael Handford, Hilary Herbert (née Lawrence), Mabel Hobbs, Mary Lim, Lionel Lock, James J.McGrane, Peter and Frances Mills, Cyril and Maureen Palmer, Graham Palmer, Marjorie Talmage, Trevor Tiplady, Gill Watts, Dennis White, Ena Wordsworth and Geoff Worrall. I would also like to thank Michael Marshman and Judith Blades of Wiltshire County Council Local Studies Library for permission to use photos from their Frith Collection, as well as the following photographic studios: Chapman and Son, Mayotte, A.Parsons and Tomkins and Barrett.

I am also indebted to Wendy Bann, Margaret Chaplin, Denis Holland, Edward Judge, Hugh Stancliffe, David Stevens and John Dennis and his staff at The Crowood Press, Ramsbury, for help in production.

Finally, and most importantly, I thank my husband, Duncan, whose photographic expertise, both in taking many of the pictures and processing and printing them, made the creation of this book possible.

(*Left*) G.Wren, the hardware shop,
in the High Street about 1910.

1 *Introduction*

Ramsbury is a village in Wiltshire with a population of about 1600 people. It lies in central southern England on the River Kennet, at one time on the main London to Bristol road, and now within fifteen minutes of a junction on the M4 motorway.

Probably the most flourishing time in its history was the Saxon period - it may have been named after a Saxon leader, Hraefn, hence Hraefn's burg or fortified place. Between the seventh and eighth centuries it had an iron smelting forge site, although the nearest iron ore was at Seend, near Devizes, and in the tenth century a bishopric was created. The latter joined with Sherborne in 1045 and the combined see was transferred in 1075 to Old Sarum, a manor belonging to Ramsbury Hundred which happened to be vacant at the time, before moving to Salisbury.

In the Domesday Survey of 1086, Ramsbury is listed as a well-off hundred with ten corn mills, compared for example to Newbury's two mills. The mainstay of the economy was farming. The Saxon common field system prevailed until the seventeenth century when farms began to be built away from the village and private enclosure took place round them. Full enclosure came with a Parliamentary Act for Ramsbury of 1778.

The increasing importance of the routeway brought industry and trade to the village. The area was well-suited to the brewing and tanning industries, with plentiful water from the clear chalk Kennet river, a type of soil suitable for growing barley for brewing, the wealth of beech mast from the woods and plenty of sheepskins for tanning. These advantages, combined with the means of transport, caused the village industries to flourish from the sixteenth to the eighteenth centuries. Ramsbury Ale was spoken of in the same breath as London Porters and Burton Ales.

The 1830s brought agricultural rioting by the labourers against both the introduction of machinery to farming, and their dispossession from the land with enclosure. Many from Ramsbury joined in machine breaking, the local craftsmen being the leaders. Some were transported to Van Diemen's land - now Tasmania, Australia, and have since flourished. Others went to the new industrial centres, in

Aerial view of Ramsbury in 1986.

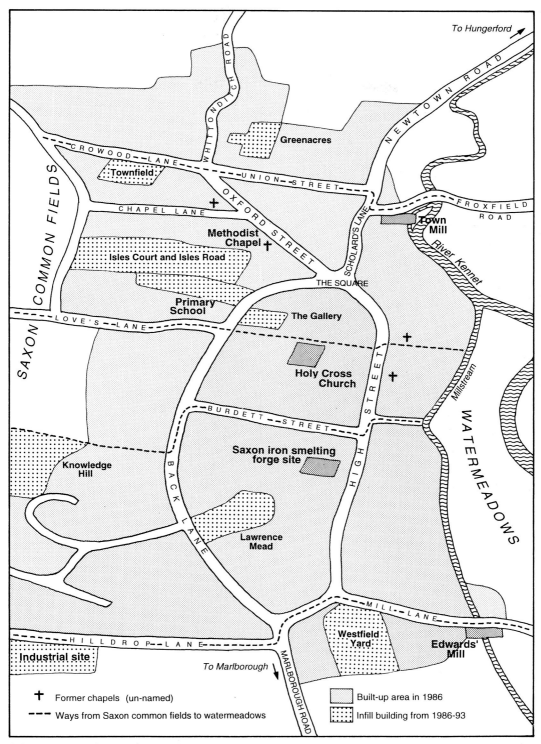

Map corresponding to the aerial view showing street names and development since 1986.

particular Swindon, with its new railway works. Yet others went to Patagonia, in South America, to join the sheep farming venture of the Waldron's from Marridge Hill.

Ramsbury had often been a place of dissent. In 1669 the curate, Henry Dent, left his post and led a non-conformist following in the village. Primitive and Wesleyan Methodists, and Congregationalists became strong forces in the community. They were led by prominent members of the village; who were also involved in tanning and brewing, the first Sunday school education, and founding the Ramsbury Building Society.

More recent dissent came in the 1980s when Ramsbury's ancient elm in the Square died, probably from a combination of old age and Dutch elm disease. Keeping the old dead tree or planting a new one split the village and for a while brought Ramsbury international fame.

The decline of tanning and brewing and their associated industries as competition increased, together with the loss of the London-Bristol route when the A4 was turnpiked in 1744, the rejection of the canal and then the railway, left Ramsbury in something of a backwater. From a peak population in 1851 of 2696 (exactly the same as Hungerford then) the numbers fell to about 1000 in 1921 as villagers left to find work elsewhere.

The two World Wars and the introduction of cars brought more mobility, while the construction of the M4 motorway in 1972, and Ramsbury's position in the 'hi-tec' industrial corridor near the hugely expanding centre of Swindon, have encouraged major development in the village. Numerous small private industries operate from Ramsbury, especially since the 1990s recession. Many work in Swindon, others work further afield, and yet more come to retire here. It is now a lively, flourishing community, with an ever increasing school, numerous clubs and societies, and, since 1974, its own bishop again.

This collection of photographs has been put together not only to complete the history of the village which was documented up to the Second World War in my book *The Village in the Valley*, but also as a pictorial record of the changes which have occurred in Ramsbury over the twentieth century. Photographing the streets in the 1990s was almost impossible because of the number of cars, so many of the more recent views are from the 1970s and 1980s.

The colour photographs were selected to illustrate the beauty of the countryside around Ramsbury and the community spirit within the village. It is a privilege to live here.

(*Above*) Ramsbury from Spring's Hill in the 1940s.

(*Below*) Ramsbury from Spring's Hill in 1995.

RAMSBURY

The dew upon the grass do lay
Heralding another dawn,
The sun rises o'er Eastridge
That's how the day is born,

In this village in the folds
of the rolling Wiltshire hills,
Beside the Kennet rippling down
the weir and through the mills.

Before the sun does rise to' far
bringing its glorious light,
The farmer in his field of corn
surveys a wonderous sight,

Birds and bees, rabbits and hares,
a fox, a pair of swans
in this quiet peaceful place
gambol or sing their songs.

Then as the sun transcends the sky
it seeks out many things,
shines down upon our tree so bold
and to our village brings

Life and vigour to us all
who live here with our friends,
We hope that sun will never set
to bring daylight to an end,

For we and others long ago
have learned this place to love,
to open up our hearts and minds
to blessings from above,

We thank all those who came before,
Who built our village here
For Ramsbury is the only place
that we hold ever dear.

CYRIL PALMER

Further down Oxford Street, in about 1914 and again in 1974. In the earlier view (*top*), the second house on the left became Hunter's haberdashery shop, now no longer trading. The first tiled house on the right was the old police house, with Penny's bakery where the bow windows are, just beyond it.

RAMSBURY, OXFORD STREET.

Oxford Street, past Chapel Lane, before the Second World War but after electricity had been put in the village in 1929.

(*Inset*) People standing by the railings outside the Methodist Church, built in 1876, and next to Hobbs the bootmakers, looking back up Oxford Street. In the main picture the Methodist Church railings can be seen lower down on the right hand side.

(*Above*) The lower part of Oxford Street in about 1910, with Ruche House on the right, once a dame school, and next to it one of two iron foundries in the village in the 1860s. Early this century, the latter became a pork butcher's shop selling locally famous sausages, before becoming a private house.

(*Right*) A similar view in 1975.

The view from Oxford Street into the Square in 1994, and also in the 1950s (*below*). Marks' fruiterer and confectioner shop and Pullen's furniture stores and 'showroom' are next to Hill's grocery shop, established in 1794.

The Square in the 1950s.

The same view *(inset)* in 1994.

Rumball's house, next to his butcher's shop, was a tannery in the eighteenth century. By 1839 it had become a full-scale brewery and Ramsbury Ale was well known throughout the country. After brewing, Rumball took over the house and shop, then it became the Oakdene Guesthouse (*bottom left*), until the Ramsbury Building Society (now Portman) moved their head office there (*bottom right*). The right hand office is currently occupied by Peter Rapson, Estate Agent.

Looking back at the Square from the High Street in 1906 and again in 1975 (*inset*). The major change since 1975 has been the planting of the oak tree in place of the elm.

Much of this centre part of Ramsbury was burnt in two fires, one in 1648 and a second in 1781, hence the lack of thatch. Ramsbury's brewing industry was the prime cause of the fires. The house with the round window was built after the 1781 fire by the vicar, who used it to house the curate. The public hall to the left was well known in the Second World War for film shows and theatre entertainment.

The 1994 view (*below*) illustrates the problems of cars in the village, otherwise little has changed except the conversion of the public hall to dwellings, called Old Theatre Place, and the addition of buildings to the right.

(*Below*) Norman Day, with Olive Winchcombe behind him, stands outside his dairy at Millstream in the High Street in the 1920s. The large white house on the right was Church House, owned by Phelps and Lawrence, the solicitors, who had a beautiful garden behind the high wall (*bottom right*). The lych gate was built as a memorial to the Waldrons of Marridge Hill who went to Patagonia in the 1860s to find work on sheep farms for the unemployed village farm labourers.

(*Above*) Evelyn House, left, was once a pub, called Angel and Bacon's after the tenants, but owned by the Ashley family, local tanners and brewers. Millstream, next to it, was variously a tanyard, malthouse, dairy and saddlery. The fellmongers, old Post Office and Building Society followed, down to Harrison's the drapers, now the Post Office.

By 1975 (*left*) most of the shops and businesses had gone except for Mills, the butchers, the Post Office and Lloyds Bank next to it.

(*Above*) Looking back up the High Street to Angel and Bacon's with its mansard roof, where the servants slept. On the left, past the painter's, is the Old Justice Room which was burnt down in 1917. It is thought many of Ramsbury's historical records may have been lost in the fire. The war memorial stands on the site now.

(*Left*) After the First World War it was decided to build a memorial hall, attached to Church House, The hall, opened in 1926, can be seen on the left in 1975.

(*Above*) Next to the large gates on the left in the 1830s was another blind house and the village workhouse. In 1776, an earlier workhouse, at the west end of the High Street, housed 70 poor people. In 1836 the workhouse was sold and the poor of Ramsbury were sent to Hungerford. The next thatched cottage was Moon's bakery in the 1900s, with the Salvation Army chapel beside it, built in 1908. Across the road, a soup kitchen for the poor and a reading room were run by the landed gentry.

(*Above*) Looking towards the west end of the High Street in about 1920. The pub, the Burdett Arms, is on the right at the entrance to Burdett Street. Previously they were called the White House and White House Lane respectively. By 1994 (*left*) the thatched cottage on the left had gone and the fire station had been built on the site. Briefly the Burdett Arms was called the Ramsbury Village Inn.

(*Below*) Burdett Street, then White House Lane, in the 1920s. In 1567 it was called Castell Wall and a plague pit was discovered on its west side.

(*Bottom right*) The High Street looking east in about 1920. The house on the left was demolished in 1976 and an archaeological dig exposed the major Saxon iron smelting site referred to in the introduction.

The steward of Ramsbury Manor, Edward Smith, lived at this house in the High Street, the Mead, at the end of the last century.

The cottages at the west end of Ramsbury have changed little since this photograph of about 1910.

The Bleeding Horse inn in about 1803 taken from a painting by Hendrick Frans de Cort. The inn and then restaurant ceased trading in 1981.

A similar view in the early 1900s.

Mill Lane with Edwards' Mill on the right in the 1950s, at the west end of Ramsbury.

Westfield Farmhouse, once the Kimber's dairy farm, is on the left, with a cottage, now no longer standing, in Mill Lane in the 1950s.

Edwards' Mill (*right*), probably on the site of one of Ramsbury's ten Domesday water mills, in about 1910. The Kennet river and millstream are still crossed only by footbridges and fords here. For many years the mill pond was a favourite place for the local children to swim.

In 1975 (*below*) the mill is obscured by trees, and a new house has been built.

(*Above*) Another of the Domesday mill sites, known as Town Mill (*right*), lies towards the eastern end of the village. Part of the mill house is on the left with Knapp Cottage and Knapp House centre right. The thatched cottage on the right, Little Mythe, has gone. The bridge over the River Kennet was not built until the late 1880s. It is still the only road crossing of the Kennet at Ramsbury.

(*Above*) The Knapp on the left may have been named after the industry of knapping the flints which abound in the fields, for use in buildings as seen here. Centre left is the old smithy once run by Bill Watts and Little Mythe can be seen to the right. The waggonettes, owned by the Watts family, were used for transporting people and goods as here in about 1920.

3 *Farming*

Although sheep were kept round Ramsbury through the centuries, the area was not one of the major woollen trading centres as in west Wiltshire. After enclosure in 1778, though, many local farms were amalgamated and became great sheep runs. The labourers not only lost their land in the common fields, but with the widespread sheep farming combined with the introduction of machinery from the 1830s, they lost their work as well. Many went into the new industries in Swindon, especially the railway works, others went out to Patagonia in South America.

Making hurdles for sheep pens continued round Ramsbury into the 1970s. Here, in about 1947, Harry Alexander cut the hazel coppice, which is still plentiful in the local woods, to make the hurdles.

Cutting grass in the watermeadows by the River Kennet in about 1908. From as early as 1620, until the 1950s, the watermeadows were floated to produce early feed for the lambs.

(*Above*) The women helped in the fields, here on the south side of Whittonditch Road, past the Halfway. Their clothes must surely have been the inspiration for Laura Ashley!

(*Top right*) Harvesting in the same field looking across to Spring's Hill, taken in about 1908.

(*Bottom right*) Women used to walk to the field from the village bringing baskets of food for the harvesters. These two girls were obviously enjoying themselves by the stooks in about 1908.

(*Below*) During harvesting, Stephen Osmond, from the Newtown iron foundry, hired out his steam engines and threshing machines, trundling to each farm in turn.

(*Bottom*) Making ricks was another major task for the farmers. This one was at Preston Farm owned by Ted Watts.

(*Top right*) One job which both women and children were paid to do was collecting baskets of flint stones from the fields to be used in road building. Norman Day on the right, with his brother Roland, is shown here about to collect a load of flints.

(*Right*) The desperate need for work at the end of the nineteenth century until after the First World War, drove many villagers out to the Waldron's sheep ranching venture in Patagonia and the Falklands. The land was bleak and inhospitable but while most returned after their seven-year contracts, some stayed and their descendants are still there today.

(*Above*) The end of the harvest at Ambrose Farm, at the bottom of Spring's Hill in 1940, with from left: R.Rushen, J.Orchard, W.Palmer, W.R.Chamberlain, F.Hunter, Frank Hunter, F.Chamberlain, A.Hedges, Sid Mundy, boy A.Barrett.

(*Left*) All the work involved in harvesting in 1908 can be done in 1995 by one huge combine harvester. This one, at Hilldrop Farm, does the work of three combines of the 1960s as technology continues to progress.

(*Left*) Parliament Piece, so called, it is said, because Oliver Cromwell held a meeting of his Parliament in a field adjacent to the house, was built in Charles I's reign. From the 1850s the Batson family, with nine sons and three daughters, played a major role in the social and educational activities of Ramsbury. They were fully involved in the school run by the Meyricks at Bodorgan and the vicarage, and they helped with evening classes and soup kitchens for the villagers.

(*Below*) Bodorgan, now Ramsbury Hill, in Back Lane, was built in the early eighteenth century. In the 1830s it became an overflow for the Meyrick school, under Arthur Meyrick - its stables being regarded as palaces compared to some of the cottages in the village.

1944-50 Sir Oswald Moseley lived at Crowood. It is now the home of John Dennis and The Crowood Press.

(*Bottom left*) Hilldrop Farm to the north of Ramsbury is on the site of an ancient settlement. The reeve of Ramsbury Hundred lived there in 1292. More recently, Hilldrop was part of the estate owned by the Batson family who lived at Parliament Piece, in Back Lane. It was until recently farmed by Christopher Eliot-Cohen.

The Cedars, in Scholard's Lane, was built in the eighteenth century. Once a school, when known as Hurles House, it was then home for the village solicitor, F.B.Rowland, before a wealthy engineer A.E.Oakes bought it. Oakes gave outings for the local school girls, and his wife ran a spinning industry for local women to relieve their poverty. Puffins Nursery School was started in 1993 by the present owner, Ros Fitton.

(Below) The Old Vicarage, shown here in 1985, was built in 1839. The vicarage it replaced was set up as a school when the Revd Edward Meyrick came from Hungerford to become vicar of Ramsbury in 1785. The school flourished at the vicarage and at Bodorgan until 1851. A new vicarage was built in 1965.

(Right) The Limes, in Oxford Street, was once the home of Kenneth Bilbrough, whose father owned a fleet of clipper ships and then developed his business into marine insurance. Here, Kenneth's wife, Ethel, sits at the front door in the 1940s.

5 Church and chapels

Holy Cross, Ramsbury, the parish church, was built during the thirteenth and fourteenth centuries, on the site of the Saxon cathedral minster. By 1891 it had fallen into such a terrible state of repair that a full restoration was vital. It cost £6000 and money was raised by subscriptions, fund-raising bazaars at the Manor and Littlecote, and donations including £1000 from the philanthropic Baroness Burdett-Coutts, youngest daughter of Sir Francis Burdett, 5th Baronet of Ramsbury Manor, and heiress to the Coutts banking fortune.

(*Above*) Before restoration, the church contained box pews, each allocated to families and houses in the village. The Burdetts of the Manor, for example, sat in the chancel. The pulpit was on the left, and the east window is partly obscured.

The north-west corner was set aside for the font and the midwives. Part of the singers' gallery, which ran across the west end of the church, can be seen at the top of the picture.

ELLEN SIMS

At church on Zumday marnens
We'm done up in our best
The wimmen wi' posh 'ats on
An fair-to-middlen dressed -
All easen thic-ways an' 'athirt
An' squiggen at the rest!
But Ellen Sims d'come in black,
And she do wear a little 'at
And she do zet down - at the back.

When prayers comes sart o'longish,
We elbows on me knees
I wunders what's for dinner:
I thinks about me bees.
I years the spadgers quorlen
Up ther inzide the eaves.
But Ellen Sims right down do bend
Nor zets back up on zeat agen
Till we've all zed the last 'AMEN'!

When Parson's up in pulpit
And he do bummle on
'Bout things as I cain't unnerstand
An' volks as deid an' gone,
'Owever shart 'is sermon be
To me, 'tis tarblish long!
But Ellen Sims d'zet like wood
As if she's yearen' zummat good -
An' zets there still, when we'm all stood!

And when 'tis all got owver,
We 'angs about outzide
Whiles wimmen volk do chatter,
And there we 'as to bide
'Till they can yarn wi' Squoire's wife,
Or Parson comes long-zide.
But Ellen Sims d'pass between
That quiet, she bean't 'ardly zeen.
... And some dun't even knaw she's been!

The south wall had to be completely demolished. Here we see the St Helena Chapel open to the elements. When removing the wall, a Saxon cross and stones were discovered, used as building material. The Saxon artefacts are now displayed in the former midwives' corner.

(*Above*) The church in 1910 before the present pew seating had been put in.

(*Left*) The Revd Bertie Treasure at the altar in the early 1950s.

(*Above*) From the 1660s non-conformism was strong in Ramsbury, led by Henry Dent, a former curate. John Wesley often visited the village, staying at Park Farm, and preached in 1775 and 1777, while Dr Coke tried to preach under the elm in the Square, but was attacked by villagers. The first proper Primitive Methodist chapel was built in 1842, shown here, in Chapel Lane.

(*Left*) The Wesleyan Methodists built their own chapel in the High Street but when attendance declined and they joined the Primitive Methodists in 1944, the chapel was sold and used as a scout hall. It is now in private ownership.

(*Above*) The Congregationalists also became strong in Ramsbury and in 1839 built their chapel, with a manse (the white house) adjacent to it, and a schoolroom behind. John Audley Harrison, who ran the draper's shop, led the congregation from 1843 until 1877. He was also a founder member of the Ramsbury Building Society. Regular services ceased in 1952 and in 1982 the chapel was sold.

Primitive Methodism increased in strength and a new chapel was built, in Oxford Street, in 1876. It was refurbished in 1988.

6 *The Tree*

Now it's gone, the Ramsbury Tree,
No longer there for folks to see,
Gone this piece of history,
A meeting place for you and me.
In its place an oak to be,
A very fine tree, tall and slender.
But the burning question
to me,
About that lovely old
hollow tree,
Is, can the village overwhelm
The witch's curse on the
Ramsbury Elm?

LIONEL LOCK

Ramsbury's old elm tree was referred to in 1775, as reaching the houses on the south side of the Square, suggesting it could have been about 100 years old by then. So in 1983 when it died, it might have reached the normal lifespan of an elm of 300 years.

The infants, with their teachers, outside the Board school in about 1906.

Headmaster H.J.Griffith with his class in 1954: *back* B.Davies, S.Penny, J.Martin, J.Huntley, P.Truster, M.Smith, M.Chamberlain, P.Foster, L.Chamberlain, K.Bavin *centre* T.Smith, - , A.Griffiths, P.Herring, W.Mildenhall, D.Whittington, V.Read, J.White, T.Millard, S.Grooby, R.Skuse *front* P.Humphries, G.Sheppard, F.Tracy, B.Talmage, S.Alder, -.Light, N.Watts, L.Trotman, P.Evill, R.Mills, R.Woolford, J.Addison.

The old girls' school built by Miss Read of Crowood in 1855, with the mistress's house adjacent to it. In 1903 the girls joined the boys at the Board school, and the building became variously a market garden, pottery and art gallery before being sold and developed as private housing.

The old Board (primary) school was far too small by 1987 so, in a land deal with a developer, it was demolished and replaced with a new building. The foundation stone was laid by Jack Ainslie, Chairman, Wiltshire County Council, helped by the headmistress Hilary Dodd, and pupils.

(*Right*) For nearly a year the school was temporarily housed in mobiles on the Whittonditch Road playing field.

The old school and new vicarage in 1975.

The new primary school was completed in the summer of 1988. At the same time the developer, Beechcroft, built Isles Court, sheltered housing for the elderly, and a further twenty houses in Isles Road. This was all part of the policy of allowing infilling only in Ramsbury by Kennet District Council within the area of the village plan.

Juma Lance, a teacher at the school for 34 years, was headmistress during the building. Here she receives a gift on her retirement at the end of the summer term, 1988, in the new school hall.

Trees were planted to commemorate the new school in the autumn of 1988. Dr Michael Handford holds his field maple tree steady as his wife, Jane, and the new headmaster Richard Colley, look on.

8 Shops, offices and pubs

(*Above*) Ramsbury had many more shops in the 1930s than now. The hardware stores on the left still exists, but the confectioners and tea shop next to it no longer trades. As always, the Bell Inn behind the tree, dominates most views of the Square. The bailiff of the Hundred, Thomas Popejoy, ran it in the 1750s. He had all the animals from the common fields branded with Ramsbury Town mark in his yard. An enclosed room with a gaol door in the pub may have been the local lock-up. It was removed in the 1980s.

(*Right*) Windsor House, head office of the Arab Horse Society, in the Square, was once a pub. In 1673 it was called the Swan, later the Green Dragon and in coronation year 1937 the Windsor Castle Hotel. The newsagents next to it gave up in 1979.

Burford's sweetshop and tobacconist in Oxford Street later became a shoe repair shop before becoming a private house.

(*Left*) George Chamberlain's grocery shop and delivery waggon served the west end of the High Street at the beginning of the twentieth century.

(*Below*) Franklin's, the butcher, was once a fellmonger where animal skins were made ready for the tanning process. It is still a butcher's shop, now called D.S.Mills and run in 1995 by Gilbert Mills.

A number of farms, such as Kimber's at Westfield Farmhouse, delivered milk for many years. Roland Day is seen here opposite his dairy at Millstream, about to start his delivery.

Two garages set up in the village, the Laurel's (White's) garage in Back Lane, and Central garage seen here (*left*), which was built on the site of the Church House garden in the High Street. It ceased trading in 1986.

(*Below left*) John German Estate Agents of Ashby-de-la-Zouch, set up in Ramsbury to take care of the Burdett estate at the Manor as they also looked after the Burdett's Foremark estate in Derbyshire. The staff are seen here in 1962: *back* T.Smith, K.Evill, P.Harris, T.Stokes, R.Hicklin, K.James; *centre* A.West, D.Baker, F.Wilson, D.Roberts, M.Adeley, P.Courtman, J.Cramsie; *front* M.Epson, V.Smith, V.Latcham, G.Doore.

(*Right*) The church parish magazine of 1942 gives some idea of the services and shops in the village at that time.

[67]

RAMSBURY BUILDING SOCIETY

is the oldest Building Society in the West of England, and throughout its existence of nearly a Century no Investor has ever failed to receive interest when due or lost one penny of capital.

Assets - £546,682
Reserve Fund £32,521

Investments received from 5/- to £5,000

Interest 3½% **free of Income Tax** on shares equal to £5.12.0.% with Tax at 7/6d.

Interest 3% **free of Income Tax** or shares equal to £4.16.0.% with Tax at 7/6d.

A NON-FLUCTUATING INVESTMENT.

LIBERAL ADVANCES FOR HOUSE PURCHASE.

Repayments spread over terms of from 5 to 23¼ years.

During the past four years the Society has advanced over £500,000 for House Purchase principally to Owner-occupiers.

Further particulars may be obtained from the Secretary—

H. R. CHAMBERLAIN, 8, High Street, Ramsbury.
R. J. COX, Manager Swindon Branch Office, 29a, Wood Street, Swindon.

AGENCIES:

Aldbourne - -	T. E. HOBBS, at Beaconsfield Cottage.
Marlborough & Burbage -	VINES & PINNIGER.
Hungerford - -	W. WHITE, Church Street.
London - -	F. J. HEDGES, 126 Crossbrook St., Waltham Cross, N.
Marlborough - -	A. J. H. VILE, Hazlewood, Blowhorn Street.
Newbury - -	DAY, SHERGOLD & HERBERT.
do. - -	THAKE & PAGINTON, Bartholomew Street.
Reading - -	T. G. COOK, A.C.A., 16 Friar Street.

(Above) The Ramsbury Building Society was begun in the village in 1846 as the Provident Union Building and Investment Society. It moved from 8 High Street to the Square and in 1958 still only employed five people. This advertisement is dated 1940. But then it took off, and after numerous mergers and name changes it is now the Portman Building Society, with its head office in Bournemouth.

(Right) The Boot was once owned by John Schollar, hence Scholard's Lane. It was the first pub the American airmen reached when they came to the village from the airfield on Spring's Hill during the Second World War.

(Above) The Halfway in Whittonditch Road ceased trading as a pub in the 1950s.

(*Right*) The Malt Shovel
was a malthouse in 1839
and ceased trading as a
pub in 1987.

9 Industries

(*Above*) The Old Tannery, the first house on the right, in the High Street, with the currier's house next to it, was owned and run by the Ashley family. Tanning continued here until the 1890s.

(*Right*) The tan pits could still be seen in the garden of the Old Tannery in the 1980s and the barn seen here was used to store beech mast or oak bark for producing tanning 'liquor'.

(*Left*) Stephen Osmond's iron foundry in the Newtown Road supplied all types of machinery and tools to the farming community. It operated from the 1840s to the 1920s. It was a favourite game of the local lads to mess up the moulds which were prepared for the molten iron to be poured into.

(*Right*) Blacksmiths were also vital for supplying smaller tools and, of course, shoeing horses. Bill Watts is seen here outside his smithy (later the Studio) opposite the Knapp, in about 1900. It was a lovely warm spot in the winter for the old villagers to gather.

Mrs Louie Oakes at the Cedars set up a spinning and weaving industry to help the village women earn money to alleviate their poverty.

(*Left*) The chalk streams around Ramsbury were ideal for growing watercress. Beds along the Whitton stream provided large quantities of cress in the 1930s. It was packed at the Beeches, Whittonditch, home of the Woottons who ran the industry. It was sent by rail all round the country.

(*Right*) Peter Holdsworth set up a pottery after the Second World War producing practical and decorative domestic items, with slipware designs. Here he is working with his wife, Kathy, at the old girls' school, Back Lane in 1952. The pottery was exported overseas but production ceased on his death in 1967.

(*Bottom right*) MSB, a medical supplies company owned by Cliff Andrews, is one of Ramsbury's new small industries. It began in the village but needed to expand so a disused industrial site at the west end of Ramsbury was cleared and permission was granted for the two buildings seen here. Knowledge Technology and Esperan also occupy parts of the buildings.

[72]

10 *The World Wars*

(*Above*) Casualties of the First World War came to the Old Vicarage, Back Lane (page 49) to be nursed back to health by the local VAD nurses.

Left) A great welcome home party was given to Ramsbury survivors from the First World War in the Church Room, Back Lane. In the Second War the room was used as a British restaurant.

(*Above*) A fancy-dress
cricket match was played
to celebrate the end of the
First World War. Specta-
tors sit outside the pavilion
on the Horse Race between
the village and the Manor
grounds.

(*Right*) Life continued as
normally as possible
during the wars. Local
excitement was caused
when Sir Francis Burdett's
car went into the river near
Knighton. One of
Osmond's steam engines
was used to haul it out.

(*Top right*) Men of
Ramsbury who joined
the Home Guard in the
Second World War
photographed outside
the school.

(*Centre right*) Second
World War civil defence
volunteers from the
village.

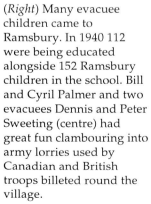

(*Right*) Many evacuee children came to Ramsbury. In 1940 112 were being educated alongside 152 Ramsbury children in the school. Bill and Cyril Palmer and two evacuees Dennis and Peter Sweeting (centre) had great fun clambouring into army lorries used by Canadian and British troops billeted round the village.

Fund raising was a major task during the Second World War. This coffee morning with Marjorie Talmage, Mrs Lawrence, Olive Winchcombe, Mrs Lewington, Mrs Sid Chamberlain and Frank Hunter was held at Elmdown Farm on 13 September 1940.

(*Centre right*) Ramsbury Section of Police Special Constables in 1941.
(*Below*) The war memorial was erected on the site of the Old Justice Room in 1926. Villagers gathered, in 1993, round the memorial before the Remembrance Day service in Holy Cross church.

11 *Clubs and societies*

(*Above*) The Ramsbury horticultural society has flourished through the twentieth century. Marjorie, Lady Burdett-Fisher, opened the annual show in 1962, assisted by F.Grooby, D.Carter, D.Mills, C.Eliot-Cohen, Dr W.T.Mills and F.Hicklin.

(*Left*) Lord Rootes, who lived at Ramsbury Manor between 1958 and 1964, was presented with a gift by Alison Palmer, after he gave out prizes at the 1963 horticultural show.

(*Top left*) A girls' club flourished in the 1930s, with outings such as this one as part of the fun.

(*Bottom left*) The Mothers' Union have always met regularly. Here they enjoy a day out in the 1950s.

(*Top right*) The football team continues to be a strong fixture in Ramsbury. This was the team and supporters of 1922-3 with: *back* Revd Shuttlecock, A.Rushen, G.Chamberlain, L.Evill, - , F.Smith, C.Winchcombe, S.Newman *centre* R.Nicklos, -.Hitchman, S.Smith, - , R.Dixon, R.Rushen *front* G.Alder, N.Hunter.

(*Centre right*) The scouts in 1926 were looked after by Miss J.Wilson, Miss E.New and Miss M.Wilson.

(*Bottom right*) From 1950 to 1982 Skipper Dewick was the Scoutmaster at Ramsbury. Here he leads the Cubs' Silver Jubilee parade through the High Street, assisted by Mrs Ricks.

The Brownies have also met at times. This was the pack in about 1937.

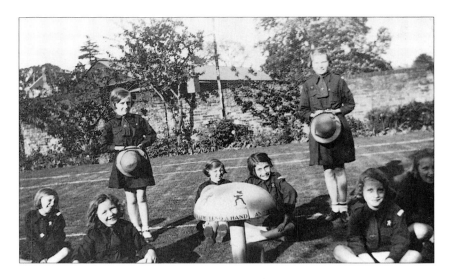

The Women's Institute celebrated their 70th anniversary in Ramsbury in 1990. The photograph shows some of them on an outing in 1959 to Claverton Manor, Bath.

(*Right*) The Silver Threads are also part of village life. Dorothy Mills presided in 1979 over their 25th anniversary party with, on her left, Nan Osmond, -, Mrs Smith, Marguerite Holmes, Florrie Newman, on her right, Mrs Bancroft, Mrs Alexander, Mrs Braxton and Mrs Low.

Ramsbury Silver Band was established in 1900. Members are shown here with their new uniforms in the 1950s: *Back* J.Bull, B.Hunter, G.Chamberlain *centre* R.Dixon, N.Hunter, J.Stroud, B.Dixon, P.West, N.Wootton, S.Hunter, E.Hobbs *front* J.Lawrence, D.Hobbs, J.Franklin, P.Hobbs, H.Hobbs, F.Edwards, B.Giddings.

(*Left*) For many years Ramsbury's Red Cross has manned an ambulance, run classes in the village and supplied Red Cross cover at local events.

(*Right*) The Young Wives' group, which met in the 1970s and 1980s, was represented at the Silver Jubilee carnival in 1976. Mary Worrall, Frances Mills, Doris Measures, Liz Hawes, Jackie Gloyne, June Bull, Babs Sparrow, Rena Plenderleith and Jenny Davison were among them.

(*Right*) The Bowls Club
has a bowling green
behind the Building
Society in the Square.
Their August Bank
Holiday fête is a highlight
of the year, as in 1993.

(*Below left*) The recreation
ground at the west end of
the village is home to the
cricket, football and tennis
clubs. A new pavilion was
opened in 1993 by David
Lawrence, Gloucester and
England cricketer, with
Ian Smith (standing),
Chairman of the Recreation
Committee, looking on.

(*Right*) The British Legion
in Ramsbury has had a
strong membership over
the years. The Ramsbury
Silver Band preceded the
Legion down the High
Street to the church for a
service in 1993 to com-
memorate the 70th
anniversary of the
Ramsbury branch.

12 *Village amenities*

One of Ramsbury's early Red Cross ambulances.

(*Right*) The firemen and engine in action in Back Lane in the 1950s.

(*Far right*) Fire appliances used to be kept under the Parish church tower in what is now the vestry. A nissan hut was built in the High Street, originally as an American-style NAAFI in the Second World War, but then used to house the engine. This was demolished and a new fire station was built on the site in 1972. The Cubs are seen here passing the nissan hut in the 1950s.

(*Above*) Captain Hill, whose family ran Hill's grocery shop, was a member of the brigade at Ramsbury around the time of the First World War.

(*Top right*) Ramsbury firefighters in 1979-80: *back* S.Harris, T.Derrick, R.Doore, P.Mills, A. Fraser, L.Hall *front* T.Pope, C.West-Oram, T.Barrett, B.Satterthwaite, M.Lockey, C.Martin.

(*Right*) Members of the Amenity Group gather for a photograph after planting their 500th tree in the village, in 1992.

(*Top right*) In 1961, 1971, 1972, 1982 and 1986 Ramsbury won the Best Kept Large Village in Wiltshire award from CPRE. David Hobbs, Chairman of Ramsbury Parish Council in 1971, accepted the award. One member of the public found the proceedings rather boring.

(*Centre right*) Mr Oakes of the Cedars, at the back, took schoolgirls on an outing in the 1930s' version of the *Ramsbury Flyer*.

(*Left*) The Community Bus, the *Ramsbury Flyer*, was inaugurated in the Square in 1993 by Edward Judge, Parish Council representative for the bus.

13 Beating the Bounds

(*Above*) In 1968 the ancient custom of beating the parish bounds was reinstituted. Here, in 1970, the first walkers, Graham Edwards, Anne Tiplady, Joan Jones, Trevor Tiplady, Peter Rapson, Viv Jones and their children stop for a photograph. The 26-mile Saxon boundary is marked by a ditch and bank over much of its length.

(*Botton left*) In 1974, the Rector, Canon Jack Davies, blessed the walkers who collected in the Square at 7.30 a.m. to be ferried to the start at Littlecote. The walk is usually completed by about 6.30 p.m.

(*Above*) The lunchtime stop at the top of Hilldrop Lane is welcome relief. Over 100 adults and children now usually take part.

(*Right*) Markers, like this sarsen stone between Aldbourne and Ramsbury, have been erected along the boundary. In 1993 the twelfth Bishop of Ramsbury, Peter Vaughan, blessed the stone, and with his wife, Elizabeth, joined the walk with the vicar, Bob Hyatt, his wife Helen, and Trevor Tiplady.

14 *Celebrations*

(*Left and below*) Queen Victoria's Golden Jubilee was celebrated in Ramsbury with a free public dinner for 1,790 people in the Board school playground. Large quantities of beef, bread, beer and plum pudding were consumed. The girls' school and mistress's house can be seen across the road.

The Methodists greatly enjoyed their outings. This photograph shows them outside the Oxford Street chapel in about 1908, with some of the waggons needed for transport.

Left) Dancing round the maypole on May Day behind the girls' school in about 1910.

(*Right*) The major event of the year was the carnival to raise funds for Savernake Hospital, Marlborough. The procession passed through the Square on 18 July 1914.

(*Above*) The Day's built a rick on a waggon at Whittonditch to join in the carnival procession in the 1930s.

(*Right*) Souvenir programme of events in Ramsbury to celebrate the Coronation in May 1937 of King George VI and Queen Elizabeth.

(*Below*) Some of the King George VI Coronation committee members outside the Bell in 1937. These men were the leading members of the village at the time, including H.G. Ludlow who was headmaster of the school from 1928 - 1953.

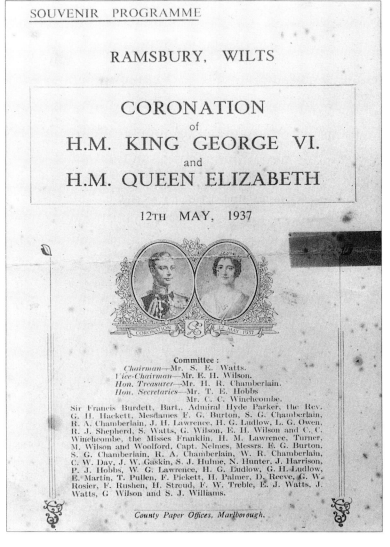

SOUVENIR PROGRAMME

RAMSBURY, WILTS

CORONATION
of
H.M. KING GEORGE VI.
and
H.M. QUEEN ELIZABETH

12TH MAY, 1937

Committee :
Chairman—Mr. S. E. Watts.
Vice-Chairman—Mr. E. H. Wilson.
Hon. Treasurer—Mr. H. R. Chamberlain.
Hon. Secretaries—Mr. T. E. Hobbs
Mr. C. C. Winchcombe.
Sir Francis Burdett, Bart., Admiral Hyde Parker, the Rev. G. H. Hackett, Mesdames F. G. Burton, S. G. Chamberlain, R. A. Chamberlain, J. H. Lawrence, H. G. Ludlow, L. G. Owen, R. J. Shepherd, S. Watts, G. Wilson, E. H. Wilson and C. C. Winchcombe, the Misses Franklin, H. M. Lawrence, Turner, M. Wilson and Woolford, Capt. Nelmes, Messrs. F. G. Burton, S. G. Chamberlain, R. A. Chamberlain, W. R. Chamberlain, C. W. Day, J. W. Gaskin, S. J. Hulme, N. Hunter, J. Harrison, P. J. Hobbs, W. G. Lawrence, H. G. Ludlow, G. H. Ludlow, E. Martin, T. Pullen, F. Pickett, H. Palmer, D. Reeve, G. W. Rosier, F. Rushen, H. Stroud, F. W. Treble, E. J. Watts, J. Watts, G. Wilson and S. J. Williams.

County Paper Offices, Marlborough.

S.Williams E.Hobbs P.Hobbs G.Rosier Ludlow D.Reeve Hunter F.Treble J.Gaskin E.Watts - H.G.Ludlow C.C.Winchcombe
S.Watts C.Day W.Nightingale J.Harrison H.Palmer E.Lawrence T.Pullen F.Rushen F.G.Burton S.G.Chamberlain

(*Above*) Queen Elizabeth II's Silver Jubilee in June 1977 followed the same format of celebrations in Ramsbury as for Queen Victoria's Golden Jubilee. One event in the morning was the tug-o'-war across the River Kennet at Mill Lane, with suitable duckings for the losers!

(*Left*) The Town Crier, Ronnie Price, in full regalia including the raven badge of office, during the 1977 Jubilee day of celebrations.

(*Above*) The afternoon carnival procession included the author's husband, Duncan, in Edwardian costume, with Ena Wordsworth and Peter Rapson, representing the tennis club.

Instead of a feast for the whole village, there was tea for all the children, with tables stretching down the High Street. Afterwards each child was presented with a commemorative mug made by Kathy Holdsworth.

(*Right*) A Donkey Derby is always popular in the village. This one took place in 1994 on the recreation ground at the west end of Ramsbury.

(*Bottom right*) The Recreation Centre committee raises funds each year with a street fair. It is possible to close the High Street because Back Lane can be used as an alternative route. The clown on stilts reminds us of Charlie, a son of the vicar, Dr Edward Graves Meyrick, who was always laughing and merry. He caused the villagers much amusement as he paraded the streets of Ramsbury in the 1830s on his ten foot high stilts, no mean feat on the flint-strewn roads. The streets have changed but the village spirit continues on through the centuries.

15 *A living village*

An aerial view of the centre of Ramsbury, looking east, in
1986 before the old elm tree was replaced by an English oak.

Holy Cross Parish church in the spring set off by a carpet of primroses and daffodils.

Bluebells flourish in the chalk woodlands, as here near Hilldrop Farm.

High summer looking across the watermeadows to Rachel's Cottage and Spring's Hill beyond.

Late autumn at the top of Hilldrop Lane is reminiscent of a Roland Hilder landscape.

The River Kennet from the Froxfield Road bridge after a hard winter frost.

Ramsbury in the beautiful valley of the River Kennet, taken from Spring's Hill in 1995.

The annual Scout fête is held by kind permission of John and Rosemary Pinches
in Parliament Piece gardens. This one was in 1993.

The soap box Derby held on Jubilee day 1977.
Cyril Palmer and Michael Watts with their sons,
Shaun and Andrew, fight for first place.

The new oak tree presided over the 1994 street fair.

Ramsbury Manor in 1995.

The village in winter snow from Mill Lane.